Pickup Trucks

by Derek Zobel

BELLWETHER MEDIA • MINNEAPOLIS, MN

Note to Librarians, Teachers, and Parents:

Blastoff! Readers are carefully developed by literacy experts and combine standards-based content with developmentally appropriate text.

Level 1 provides the most support through repetition of high-frequency words, light text, predictable sentence patterns, and strong visual support.

Level 2 offers early readers a bit more challenge through varied simple sentences, increased text load, and less repetition of high-frequency words.

Level 3 advances early-fluent readers toward fluency through increased text and concept load, less reliance on visuals, longer sentences, and more literary language.

Level 4 builds reading stamina by providing more text per page, increased use of punctuation, greater variation in sentence patterns, and increasingly challenging vocabulary.

Level 5 encourages children to move from "learning to read" to "reading to learn" by providing even more text, varied writing styles, and less familiar topics.

Whichever book is right for your reader, Blastoff! Readers are the perfect books to build confidence and encourage a love of reading that will last a lifetime!

This edition first published in 2009 by Bellwether Media, Inc.

No part of this publication may be reproduced in whole or in part without written permission of the publisher. For information regarding permission, write to Bellwether Media, Inc., Attention: Permissions Department, Post Office Box 19349, Minneapolis, MN 55419.

Library of Congress Cataloging-in-Publication Data
Zobel, Derek, 1983–
  Pickup trucks / by Derek Zobel.
    p. cm. – (Blastoff! readers: Mighty machines)
  Includes bibliographical references and index.
  Summary: "Simple text and full color photographs introduce young readers to pickup trucks. Intended for students in kindergarten through third grade"–Provided by publisher.
  ISBN-13: 978-1-60014-236-9 (hardcover : alk. paper)
  ISBN-10: 1-60014-236-2 (hardcover : alk. paper)
  1. Pickup trucks–Juvenile literature. I. Title.

TL230.5.P49Z624 2009
629.223'2-dc22   2008033100

Contents

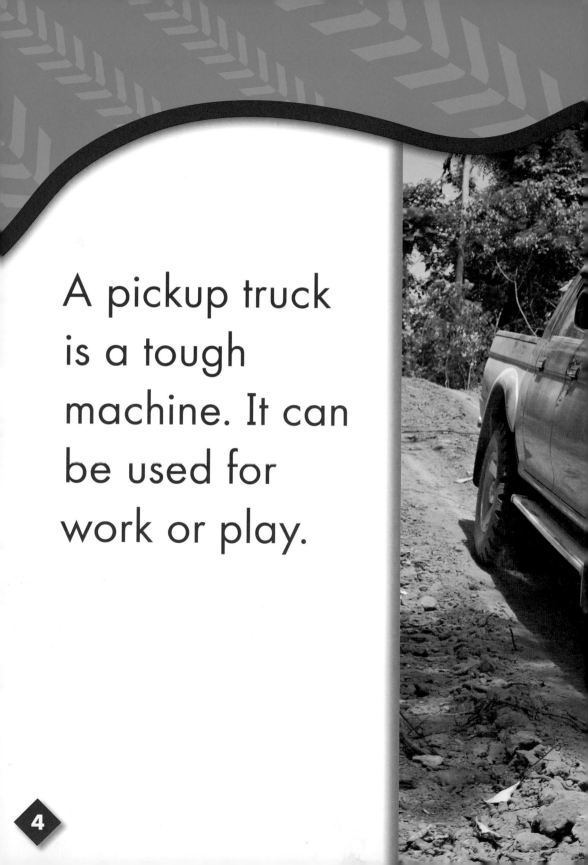

A pickup truck is a tough machine. It can be used for work or play.

A pickup truck has a **cab**. The driver sits in the cab.

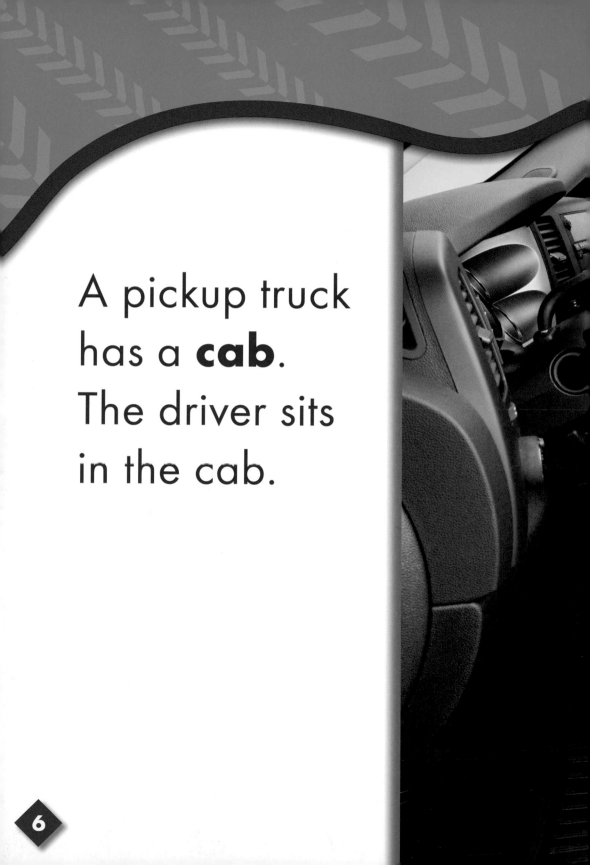

A pickup truck has an **engine**. The engine gives the truck power.

A pickup truck has a **bed**. **Cargo** goes in the bed.

bed

This red
pickup truck
carries rocks.

Some pickup trucks have a **hitch**. They can **tow** things.

hitch

This pickup
truck tows
a **camper**.

This pickup truck tows a **trailer**. The trailer carries horses.

This pickup truck tows a boat. Have fun!

Glossary

bed—the part of a pickup truck that holds cargo

cab—the place where the driver of a vehicle sits

camper—a place where people can cook meals and sleep; campers can be towed or fit over the bed of a pickup truck.

cargo—loads carried by trucks, ships, trains, or planes

engine—a machine that makes a vehicle move

hitch—a part on the back of a pickup truck; trailers hook up to the hitch.

tow—to pull something

trailer—a vehicle that can be towed by a car or truck; trailers carry cargo.

To Learn More

AT THE LIBRARY
Gere, Bill. *The Truck Book*. Racine, Wisc.:
Golden Books, 1997.

Wheeler, Lisa. *Farmer Dale's Red Pickup Truck*.
Orlando, Fla.: Harcourt, 2006.

Zuehlke, Jeffrey. *Pickup Trucks*. Minneapolis,
Minn.: Lerner, 2007.

ON THE WEB
Learning more about mighty
machines is as easy as 1, 2, 3.

1. Go to www.factsurfer.com.

2. Enter "mighty machines" into the search box.

3. Click the "Surf" button and you will see a list
   of related Web sites.

With factsurfer.com, finding more information
is just a click away.

Index

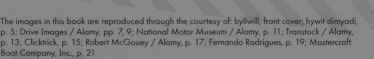

The images in this book are reproduced through the courtesy of: byllwill, front cover; hywit dimyadi, p. 5; Drive Images / Alamy, pp. 7, 9; National Motor Museum / Alamy, p. 11; Transtock / Alamy, p. 13; Clicktrick, p. 15; Robert McGouey / Alamy, p. 17; Fernando Rodrigues, p. 19; Mastercraft Boat Company, Inc., p. 21.